Experiencing Poetry

Poems About
Emotions

Clare Constant

Heinemann
LIBRARY
Chicago, Illinois

Text © 2014 Heinemann Library
an imprint of Capstone Global Library, LLC
Chicago, Illinois
First published in hardback in 2014
Paperback edition first published in 2015

To contact Capstone Global Library please
phone 800-747-4992, or visit our website www.
capstonepub.com

Produced for Raintree by
White-Thomson Publishing

www.wtpub.co.uk
+44 (0)843 208 7460

Edited by Alice Harman
Cover design by Tim Mayer
Designed by Alix Wood
Concept design by Alix Wood
Original illustrations © Capstone Global
Library Ltd 2014

Production by Victoria Fitzgerald
Originated by Capstone Global Library Ltd
Printed and bound in China

**Library of Congress Cataloging in
Publication Data**
Experiencing Poetry : Poems About Emotions
/ [compiled and edited by] Clare Constant.
    pages cm.—(Experiencing poetry)
  Includes bibliographical references and
index.
  ISBN 978-1-4329-9556-0 (hb)—
ISBN 978-1-4329-9563-8 (pb) 1. English
poetry. 2. American poetry. 3. Poetry—
Authorship. 4. Poetry—Explication.
I. Constant, Clare, editor of compilation.
II. Title. III. Title: Oranges and other poems
about emotions.
  PN6110.E5E97 2014
  808.81'9353—dc23 2013018335

17 16 15 14 13
10 9 8 7 6 5 4 3 2 1

Poems reproduced by permission of:
p. 8 "Oranges" by Gary Soto. From Gary Soto:
New and Selected Poems © 1995 by Gary Soto.
Used with permission of Chronicle Books
LLC, San Francisco. Visit ChronicleBooks.
com.
p. 14 "Don't Say I Said" by Sophie Hannah,
Leaving and Leaving You (Carcanet Press
Limited, 1995).
p. 18 "nikki-rosa" by Nikki Giovanni.
Copyright © 1993. Reprinted with permission
of the author.
p. 22 "Neighbours" by Benjamin Zephaniah
(Copyright © Benjamin Zephaniah) is
reproduced by permission of United Agents
(www.unitedagents.co.uk) on behalf of
Benjamin Zephaniah.
p. 26 "As I Grew Older", from The Collected
Poems of Langston Hughes by Langston
Hughes, edited by Arnold Rampersad with
David Roessel, Associate Editor, copyright ©
1994 by the Estate of Langston Hughes. Used
by permission of Alfred A. Knopf, a division
of Random House, Inc. Any third party use
of this material, outside of this publication,
is prohibited. Interested parties must apply
directly to Random House, Inc for permission.
Also reproduced with the permission of David
Higham, in the UK.
p. 32 "Do not go gentle into that good
night" by Dylan Thomas, from The Poems
of Dylan Thomas, copyright 1952. Reprinted
by permission of New Directions Publishing
Corp. In the UK, reproduced from Dylan
Thomas, Everyman Selected Poems (J Dent,
1951).
p. 38 "Valentine" by Carol Ann Duffy.
Copyright © Carol Ann Duffy 1993.
Reproduced by permission of the author c/o
Rogers, Coleridge & White Ltd., 20 Powis
Mews, London W11 1JN.

Clare Constant would like to dedicate this
book to her amazing colleagues and students
at Thames Christian College.

Picture credits and URL disclaimer can be
found on page 63.

Every effort has been made to contact
copyright holders of any material
reproduced in this book. Any omissions
will be rectified in subsequent printings
if notice is given to the publisher.

CONTENTS

A World of Emotions

How many feelings have you experienced already today? Worry when you overslept? Relief when you still made it to school on time? Irritation at your classmates' unfunny remarks? Delight at the grade your teacher gave you? Every day is packed with emotions.

Our emotions drive our actions—both our best and worst choices. Love can prompt you to give a generous and thoughtful present; jealousy can lead you to make spiteful remarks that hurt another's feelings. Emotions are part of every experience we have, and life would be much less interesting without them. It is not surprising that poets write about emotions so much!

Good poetry can leave you with the powerful impression that you have deeply understood and shared the poet's emotions. The ideas may play and replay in your imagination. However, when you struggle to understand a poem and can't make sense of it, it can be infuriating! You may decide that poetry isn't for you, and think that you should just give up.

Don't. This book will give you keys to open doors into poetry. It will explain the techniques poets use to create certain effects, and will help you explore the meanings of different poems. There are eight poems to discover. Each is written by a different poet, and each demonstrates various techniques for expressing ideas about emotions. By the end of this book, you will know a lot more about poetry—and, perhaps, a little more about your emotions!

Reading an Image

Try this experiment to find out how you can read an image and understand it without any direct explanation. On the page opposite are two images that express different ideas about love. Study them one at a time. Note down everything you think the image is showing you about love.

All the ideas you think these images express about love are held within them—without the photographer having to explain anything to you. A picture can express so much more than just the likeness of an object. In the same way, a poem can express so much more than just what its words tell you.

Think About This
Simple but Effective

Sometimes the most powerful poems are short and seemingly simple. This is because the poet has spent hours weeding out unneeded ideas and words. The American poet Rita Dove expresses it like this:

Poetry is language at its most distilled and powerful.
(Distilled means a product has been purified or concentrated.)

Do you agree with this definition of poetry?

How to Begin Reading a Poem

Expect to read and reread a poem several times. Follow the five tips below to help you start to make sense of a poem.

1. Start with the Obvious

Focus on what you can understand first. Read the poem one sentence at a time (or each part that makes sense as a whole, if there is no punctuation). Even in the most "difficult" poem there will be words, perhaps even whole sentences, that you can make sense of.

Next, ask yourself what the whole poem might be about. Often the key **theme** (subject or thought) is likely to be expressed in the first few lines or at the end. If the poem is telling a story, ask yourself what the story is about. This should uncover some of its themes.

2. Work on What You Don't Understand

Decide which of these things is making a line difficult to read:

- **Are the sentence parts "in the wrong order"?** Try rewriting the poem, placing the same words in a different order, to see if that makes the meaning clearer.
- **Are there unfamiliar words?** Use a dictionary.
- **Is the poem describing an unfamiliar place or time?** Research it on the Internet.
- **Could it be an image?** Is the writer making a comparison to create a picture? Look at tip 4 on the opposite page to find out how to make sense of an image.

3. Record Key Details and Techniques

Once you have worked out the general message that the writer is trying to express (such as "this is what true love is like" or "this is how **prejudiced** people behave"), then record all the other details and techniques you notice. They will be helping to convey the poem's purpose and themes more precisely.

4. Make Sense of the Images

There's a saying that "a picture is worth a thousand words." The diagrams below explain how an image (word picture) works in poetry.

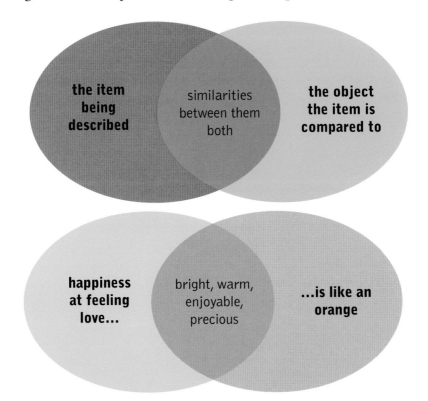

5. Note Down Any Other Techniques

Poets use lots of other techniques alongside **imagery**. You will learn more about these throughout the book, but here are the four main things to look for:

- **Associations:** These are words that hint at and suggest other things—for example, red is associated with fire, danger, and passion.
- **Sound effects: Rhythm**, **rhyme**, **alliteration**, and **onomatopoeia** are used to make the reader hear something that expresses the intended message of the poem.
- **Structure:** This describes how the poem is organized—for example, how it begins and ends, and in what order themes and other points are given (even within sentences).
- **Contrasts and similarities:** Note any opposites (such as dark and light, old and young, love and hate) or repeated words and phrases in the poem, as these often contain significant themes.

"Oranges"

G ary Soto grew up in the 1960s in the sunny state of
California, where lots of oranges are grown. In this
poem, the oranges and their warm, vivid color help Soto
express his feelings of happiness.

"Oranges"

by Gary Soto

The first time I walked
With a girl, I was twelve,
Cold, and weighted down
With two oranges in my jacket.
December. Frost cracking
Beneath my steps, my breath
Before me, then gone,
As I walked toward
Her house, the one whose
Porch light burned yellow
Night and day, in any weather.
A dog barked at me, until
She came out pulling
At her gloves, face bright
With rouge. I smiled,
Touched her shoulder, and led
Her down the street, across
A used car lot and a line
Of newly planted trees,
Until we were breathing
Before a drugstore. We
Entered, the tiny bell
Bringing a saleslady
Down a narrow aisle of goods.
I turned to the candies
Tiered like bleachers
And asked what she wanted -
Light in her eyes, a smile
Starting at the corners

Of her mouth. I fingered
A nickel in my pocket,
And when she lifted a chocolate
That cost a dime,
I didn't say anything.
I took the nickel from
My pocket, then an orange,
And set them quietly on
The counter. When I looked up,
The lady's eyes met mine,
And held them, knowing
Very well what it was all
About.

Outside,
A few cars hissing past,
Fog hanging like old
Coats between the trees.
I took my girl's hand
In mine for two blocks,
Then released it to let
Her unwrap the chocolate.
I peeled my orange
That was so bright against
The gray of December
That, from some distance,
Someone might have thought
I was making a fire in my hands.

FREE VERSE

The form of poetry in which "Oranges" is written is called **free verse**. It doesn't have a regular rhyme or rhythm pattern, nor does it have **stanzas** of a regular length. Instead, the writer ends lines on words he wants to emphasize, and changes the stanza when the characters move from inside the drugstore to outside it. The overall effect of using this form of poetry is that the poem sounds less formal—it is almost like a conversation with the reader.

GARY SOTO

1952–
Born: Fresno, California, USA

Gary Soto's parents were working-class Mexican Americans. He worked in the fields when he was young to raise some extra money for the family. When Soto was at high school, he became motivated to work hard at his studies. He went on to gain a degree and then study poetry. As well as teaching at universities in the United States, Soto has volunteered as a teacher for Spanish speakers who want to learn English.

Gary Soto has written 11 poetry collections for adults, and has also written books for children and young adults.

Did you know? Gary Soto produced a movie, *The Pool Party*, which won the 1993 Andrew Carnegie Medal for Film Excellence.

Unpeeling "Oranges"

It is time to try using the five steps described on pages 6–7. They will help you begin to understand "Oranges" more fully, and appreciate what the poet has achieved.

1. Start with the Obvious

Read and reread "Oranges" aloud one sentence at a time (ignoring the line endings) until you can sum up the basic story. Which of the ideas below do you agree with most? Why?

a. The poet is remembering he ate a delicious orange on his first date.
b. The boy has brought two oranges from home to share with his first girlfriend, and he also has a nickel. When she wants an expensive chocolate, he uses both the nickel and her orange to pay for it. Then he eats his own orange, feeling really happy.

2. Work on What You Don't Understand

Use a dictionary if there are any words you don't understand in the poem. Write down the definitions, so you can look at them again if you need to.

Do some research on Gary Soto, starting with his personal profile on page 9 of this book. You will discover that his parents did not have much money when he was young, which might help you understand why the boy in the poem only has a nickel (and an orange!) to spend. You will also see that Soto was a boy in the 1960s, quite a long time ago now, which explains why the chocolate might seem unusually cheap to young people today.

Think About This
What Is a Theme?

A theme is a subject or thought that a writer wants to explore or share with his or her readers.

After you have discovered what a poem is about, work out what the main theme is by asking yourself: What does this poem show me? After reading "Oranges," two readers might have these different interpretations of the poem:

> The poem shows readers how happy first love makes you feel.

> The poem shows that young love can overcome poverty.

It is fine for different readers to have varying ideas about the main theme of a poem. As long as you can find evidence that shows your ideas are clearly represented in the poem, your interpretation will be valid.

3. Record Key Details and Techniques

Once you have generally understood the poem, and are fairly clear about the writer's main ideas and intended themes, your next step is to reread the poem. This time, focus on the poet's choice of details, vocabulary, and techniques. These are all included to develop the ideas and themes in some way—your challenge is to discover how they do it.

4 Make Sense of the Images

There are a few images in "Oranges," so let's look at two more closely:

simile

"...the candies
Tiered like bleachers"

metaphor

"Someone might have thought
I was making a fire in my hands."

Think about what is being compared by jotting down the comparison in a diagram like the one on page 7. You could also search on the Internet for some pictures of bleachers and rows of candies in a store, and of oranges and fire. Perhaps you could create a collage of the images found in this poem. Print out the pictures you have found on the Internet, and paste them onto a page. Compare the images and see what similarities you can spot. What do you think the poet is trying to get you to notice?

Candies and bleachers: long straight lines, rising rows...
Orange and a fire: bright orange color, warmth, glow...

"A fire in my hands" sounds dangerous, so it is a memorable way to end the poem. As Soto's main idea is to describe his happiness and new love, could the fire in his hands represent his feelings in some way? (When an object represents something else, then it is acting as a **symbol**.) If he is happy with his first date and beginning to fall in love, the fire might represent his warm glow of happiness and love.

5 Note Down Any Other Techniques

In this case, let's look at associations—words that hint at or suggest more ideas. But how do you work out what a word suggests?
First, decide what the word means. For example, yellow is a color.

Then ask yourself what the word reminds most people of—not your own personal memory or ideas, but what most people would link it to (these are the word's associations). If the poet is from an unfamiliar time or culture, you may need to do some research to be certain your ideas are relevant. For instance: "Yellow reminds us of the warm Sun. It's cozy and cheerful."

Describing the girlfriend's porch light as yellow creates associations of coziness, cheerfulness, and warmth, and connects them with the girl's family.

You might like to practice working out words' associations by scanning the poem for:

- cold and warm things
- sounds
- brightness.

Think About This
How Do I Know If My Ideas Are Valid?

Test your ideas using the two questions below. As long as the answer to both questions is yes, your views are valid even if they are different from someone else's.
1. Does what you think a word or image suggests fit in with what the rest of the poem is about?
2. From what you know of other texts (poems, books, films, and so on), is this idea likely?
For example, in many texts passionate feelings of love are represented as a fire burning. The idea that the fire in the boy's hands represents his growing love is possible if it also fits in with what the rest of the poem is about. As the whole poem describes a first date when love could grow, it does fit in.

"Don't Say I Said"

The poem on page 15 is a **monologue**, which means one character is speaking to an audience. To help you understand it better, it might be fun to record yourself performing the poem on your cell phone. Then replay it, imagining you are the friend on the other end of the phone receiving the call.

Using the Five Steps

Read through the poem and then try using the five steps on pages 6–7. These steps will help you, but don't be surprised if sometimes one of the steps is less useful. For example, there is not much imagery in "Don't Say I Said."

You may have some ideas about what you think the speaker is really up to. She wants her ex-boyfriend to realize that he has lost someone amazing, and she doesn't want him to know she asked her friend to tell him that. But why? What are her feelings? Does she still love him and want him back? Or is she feeling bitter after his rejection and wanting to make sure he regrets ending it with her?

Since the poem does not clearly tell us, you have to work out what you think. Remember, as long as you can show your ideas are based on what is said in the poem, your view will be valid.

WORDS YOU MAY NOT KNOW

stone: This is the same as about 14 lb. (6 kg) in weight.
spontaneous: If something isn't planned, it is spontaneous.
grassing: This is an informal term for giving away a secret.
top-note: This is the lightest, freshest scent in a perfume.
frivolity: This means light-heartedness or silliness.
replete: To be replete is to be filled with something.
eradicated: This means completely removed or destroyed.
carp: To carp is to criticize or to nag.

"Don't Say I Said"

by Sophie Hannah

Next time you speak to you-know-who
I've got a message for him.
Tell him that I have lost a stone
Since the last time I saw him.
Tell him that I've got three new books
Coming out soon, but play it
Cool, make it sound spontaneous.
Don't say I said to say it.

He might ask if I've mentioned him.
Say I have once, in passing.
Memorise everything he says
And, no, it won't be grassing
When you repeat his words to me –
It's the only way to play it.
Tell him I'm toned and tanned and fine.
Don't say I said to say it.

Say that serenity and grace
Have taken root inside me.
My top-note is frivolity
But beneath, dark passions guide me.
Tell him I'm radiant and replete
And add that every day it
Seems I am harder to resist.
Don't say I said to say it.

Tell him that all my ancient faults
Have been eradicated.
I do not carp or analyse
As I might have when we dated.
Say I'm not bossy any more
Or, better still, convey it
Subtly, but get the point across.
Don't say I said to say it.

SOPHIE HANNAH

1971–
Born: Manchester, England

This is what **Sophie Hannah** says about her writing:

"I write in order to communicate with and entertain others, to process experience and make something lasting out of it, and in order to exercise some kind of control over life. But mainly I write because I can't imagine not writing – it's the main way in which I express myself and deal with both the good and bad aspects of life."

Sophie Hannah writes witty poems that are often about the battle of the sexes (how men and women see things differently).

Did you know? Sophie Hannah doesn't just write poetry. She also writes psychological thrillers for adults, novels for teenagers, and stories for younger children.

Noticing Patterns: Rhythm

Read "Don't Say I Said" aloud, tapping your finger as you say each syllable so that you can hear the poem's strong rhythm. Remember that everything in the poem is there for a reason. It will have taken a lot of work to make sure every line creates this pattern. So the question is: why? The answer is that it must create an effect that helps reinforce the ideas that the poet is trying to get across.

Noticing Patterns: Repetition

"Don't say I said to say it." is repeated four times in the poem, so there must be a reason for this **repetition**. By the last time, does it make the speaker seem bossy? That's the exact opposite of what she claims to be!

Rhythm and Emotion

This is a poem expressing the speaker's feelings about her situation. Having a fast rhythm with a strong beat does not make her voice sound relaxed and peaceful—it makes her sound insistent. Is she angry or desperate? Either of these feelings suits a rejected woman who wants her ex-boyfriend to know what he is missing by not being with her.

However, Hannah does more than just entertain us with an overheard conversation between a woman and her friend discussing an ex. The people are unnamed, suggesting they could be anyone, and hinting that this game-playing between men and women is common. It is up to the reader to agree or disagree with this.

WHAT IS VIEWPOINT?

In this poem, we only hear the speaker's thoughts and feelings about her ex-boyfriend and herself. This means that it is expressed from the speaker's viewpoint. In "Oranges," the date is described from the boy's **viewpoint**.

Just because the first person ("I think/do/say…") is used in a poem, do not assume that the character and the poet are the same person. Poets often create characters (called **personas**) whose views or experiences are different from their own.

"nikki-rosa"

Nikki Giovanni was 25 when she wrote this poem in 1968. It is **autobiographical** (related to the writer's own life). Read through the poem and see what you can understand by yourself. Don't forget to use the five steps from pages 6–7 to help you work out your ideas.

Think About the Context

Giovanni's childhood might be very different from yours. As you read the poem, how many differences can you find?

The only way to understand some of the things Giovanni talks about is to find out about the poem's **context**—when and where it was written, and how the experiences of its author shaped it. This means finding out about Nikki Giovanni's childhood, and the time and culture in which she grew up. Read the biography of Giovanni on page 20, and use the information in it to help you understand the poem better.

The biography boxes in this book will often tell you something about the poet that helps you understand their poem better, but when you read other poems you need to do your own research. There is a list of useful websites on page 63 to help you get started.

Think About This
Pace and Emotion

When you first looked at the poem, did the missing punctuation make it harder to read? After you read the poem a couple of times, did it make the poem's rhythm faster? When people talk about something they feel passionate about, they often speak quickly and do not pause for breath.

So could the lack of punctuation be intended to create the same effect, to give the poem a particular pace? Would Giovanni be most likely to feel upset or angry about the idea that white people would not understand how much she treasures her memories of childhood?

"nikki-rosa"

by Nikki Giovanni

childhood remembrances are always a drag
if you're Black
you always remember things like living in Woodlawn
with no inside toilet
and if you become famous or something
they never talk about how happy you were to have
your mother
all to yourself and
how good the water felt when you got your bath
from one of those
big tubs that folk in chicago barbecue in
and somehow when you talk about home
it never gets across how much you
understood their feelings
as the whole family attended meetings about
Hollydale
and even though you remember
your biographers never understand
your father's pain as he sells his stock
and another dream goes
And though you're poor it isn't poverty that
concerns you
and though they fought a lot
it isn't your father's drinking that makes any difference
but only that everybody is together and you
and your sister have happy birthdays and very good
Christmases
and I really hope no white person ever has cause
to write about me
because they never understand
Black love is Black wealth and they'll
probably talk about my hard childhood
and never understand that
all the while I was quite happy

NIKKI GIOVANNI

1943–

Born: Knoxville, Tennessee, USA

Nikki Giovanni grew up in a strongly African American area in the suburbs of Cincinnati, Ohio, at a time when it was legal to discriminate against African American people. White people were educated and housed separately from African American people.

Nikki Giovanni is a famous writer, speaker, and civil rights activist who has won numerous prestigious awards and honors.

This is called segregation. Giovanni's sister was one of the first three African American students to go to Wyoming High School, which had previously been for white students only. Racist practices prevented Giovanni's father from building a house in Hollydale, an African American housing development. He became an alcoholic.

Did you know? Giovanni's real name is Yolande Cornelia Giovanni, but her sister started calling her Nikki when she was three years old.

Notice What's Missing

This poem does not follow the usual rules of punctuation. In fact, there are only nine capital letters throughout the poem. The technique of deliberately not using capital letters where they would be expected, in order to create an effect, was developed by the popular American poet E. E. Cummings in the 1920s.

Like E. E. Cummings, Giovanni makes a deliberate choice in this poem about when and how to use capital letters, rather than following the traditional rules of grammar. She gives her racial group, "Black," a capital letter, but does not do this for the other group: "white." What do you think the significance of this could be?

Prejudice and Misunderstanding

Giovanni's childhood was partly shaped by the African American struggle for racial equality in the United States. However, in the poem Giovanni reflects on how just noting the facts about her life can give a misleading picture of her childhood. It is easy to assume that it was miserable because she was poor, her parents argued a lot, and her father, an alcoholic, was distraught when his dream failed. Instead, Giovanni says she felt happy and very loved.

One of the most striking things Giovanni says is: "Black love is Black wealth." This, she says, is something "they" (a white biographer) cannot understand (perhaps due to placing value on financial wealth rather than family bonds). So, one of the themes of this poem is racial misunderstanding and prejudice.

Think About This
What Effect Do Giovanni's Views Have on Her Readers?

You are reading this poem in the 21st century, when attitudes toward prejudice and racism have been challenged for more than 50 years. In this poem, does Giovanni seem to think differently from you about white people and black people? How do you feel about that?

"Neighbours"

Before you read a poem, it is helpful to think about its carefully chosen title and decide what it suggests to you. This poem's title is "Neighbours." Use the questions below to work out what you think this title suggests.

- What will the poem be about?
- What emotions should neighbors feel about each other?
- What kind of neighbor would you not want to live near?

Now read the poem and decide whether the ideas you expect are included.

WORDS YOU MAY NOT KNOW

dreadlocks: These are long, thin braids of hair.

tongues: In a religious or spiritual context, this means to speak in words or sounds that you do not understand, but that others may sometimes interpret.

Wailer: Bob Marley and the Wailers was a successful Jamaican band that played reggae music.

Carnival: This is a period of public celebration at a regular time each year; the word can also describe an exciting mixture of something.

Notting Hill Carnival is the largest street festival in Europe, and takes place in London every summer. It is a three-day celebration of music, dancing, and African Caribbean culture.

"Neighbours"

by Benjamin Zephaniah

I am the type you are supposed to fear
Black and foreign
Big and dreadlocks
An uneducated grass eater.

I talk in tongues
I chant at night
I appear anywhere,
I sleep with lions
And when the moon gets me
I am a Wailer.

I am moving in
Next door to you
So you can get to know me,
You will see my shadow
In the bathroom window,
My aromas will occupy
Your space,
Our ball will be in your court.
How will you feel?

You should feel good
You have been chosen.

I am the type you are supposed to love
Dark and mysterious
Tall and natural
Thinking, tea total.
I talk in schools
I sing on TV
I am in the papers,
I keep cool cats

And when the sun is shining
I go Carnival.

BENJAMIN ZEPHANIAH

1958–

Born: Birmingham, England

Benjamin Zephaniah's parents came from the Caribbean and settled in Birmingham, England. Zephaniah struggled in school because he has **dyslexia**, but by the time he was 15 his poetry was already known in the local African Caribbean and Asian communities. He left school with no qualifications and eventually ended up in prison for burglary. When he got out, Zephaniah moved to London to find a wider audience for his poetry, and published his first book of poems there. His focus on making poetry relevant and enjoyable for everyone has made him one of the UK's best-loved poets.

Benjamin Zephaniah has won numerous awards for his poetry and has been an advisor to the UK government.

Did you know? Zephaniah's earliest memories are of enjoying Jamaican food, singing and dancing to reggae music, listening to the adults telling captivating stories, and then sitting quietly playing with words and rhymes in his head.

Think About Structure

When you read a poem broken into stanzas, you will often find each stanza adds a new point, building on—or contrasting with—the previous stanza. Can you see how the poet has organized the stanzas in "Neighbours" to build each step of his argument?

The Theme of Racism

Racial tension has been a significant problem in London, Birmingham, and other areas of the UK throughout Zephaniah's life. His anger at this prejudice, and his determination that it should be overcome, are major themes in his writing. This poem explores how people **stereotype** each other. This idea is expressed in the first line, where the speaker directly addresses the reader: "I am the type you are supposed to fear."

Having aroused the reader's curiosity as to what it is about the poet's looks that causes fear, we are told he is large and black and has dreadlocks. If this makes him look "foreign," that suggests the neighbor is white and English. The word *foreign* has two meanings—coming from another country, or being different. To the neighbor, Zephaniah is both types of *foreign*.

In the final line of the first stanza, "grass eater" is an insult. *Grass* is slang for the drug marijuana. Also, animals rather than humans eat grass, hinting that the neighbor views black people as either animals or drug-users.

Prejudice and stereotyping can stop people from seeing what someone is really like.

Think About This
What Is Your Reaction?

Are you angry at the neighbor for his or her attitude? How would you feel if someone judged you in this way, without really knowing you? In the rest of the poem, Zephaniah shows how fear and ignorance are at the heart of prejudice. It is a poem designed to provoke a response from readers!

Humor

Although racism is a serious subject, Zephaniah's list of things the neighbor fears he will do—ending with "I am a Wailer" (howling like a werewolf?)—becomes so exaggerated that it is comic. Perhaps Zephaniah is showing the reader how ridiculous stereotyping and prejudice is.

Can you find any other humorous lines in the poem?

"As I Grew Older"

Over time, failure, difficulties, and discouragement make many people lose hope, give up on their dreams, and settle for something less. This is the experience that the speaker describes at the beginning of the poem below.

As you read the poem, don't forget to use all that you have learned so far, especially the five steps from pages 6–7, to help you understand it.

"As I Grew Older"

by Langston Hughes

It was a long time ago.
I have almost forgotten my dream.
But it was there then,
In front of me,
Bright like a sun–
My dream.
And then the wall rose,
Rose slowly,
Slowly,
Between me and my dream.
Rose until it touched the sky–
The wall.
Shadow.
I am black.
I lie down in the shadow.

No longer the light of my dream before me,
Above me.
Only the thick wall.
Only the shadow.
My hands!
My dark hands!
Break through the wall!
Find my dream!
Help me to shatter this darkness,
To smash this night,
To break this shadow
Into a thousand lights of sun,
Into a thousand whirling dreams
Of sun!

Making Sense of Imagery

When you read a poem with lots of visual details in it, try doodling each one or putting them all together in sequence like a movie. The aim is to try and see what the writer is showing you.

> *And then the wall rose,*
> *Rose slowly,*
> *Slowly,*
> *Between me and my dream.*
> *Rose until it touched the sky–*

Symbolism

In the poem's second reference to the Sun, the speaker says he wants:

> To break this shadow
> Into a thousand lights of sun,
> Into a thousand whirling dreams
> Of sun!

This time the Sun is not being directly compared to something else (so it is not part of a metaphor or simile). Instead, it seems to represent an idea—it is symbolic.

Note what has happened in the poem since the image of the Sun was last used: the wall has gotten in the way of the Sun, and the shadow created by the wall has stopped the speaker from seeing its light. However, in these lines, he is regaining hope. He longs for the strength to break through the wall, and for the shadow to be turned into lots of suns and more dreams of other suns. It is as if the very shadow that has stopped him can become something positive.

THE SUN AND THE WALL

There are two main images in this poem: the Sun and the wall. When a poet repeats an image, you need to check for any differences in how it is used each time. For example, the wall is rising up to separate the narrator from his dream. It casts a dark shadow over him. It is a barrier to be smashed.

One way to make sense of metaphors and similes is to draw a diagram like the one below. It can help you understand what the writer is comparing and what he or she wants the reader to notice. Start with the first image of the Sun, in lines 3–5.

the Sun | similarities: bright, in front of me | my dream

When you are sure you know what the Sun is being used to suggest the first time, read on to the next place the image appears and see if it is used differently there.

The Wall

As you reread the poem, notice everything Hughes tells you about the wall. It rose up slowly and became very big. It separated him from his dream. It cast a shadow on him, and now he wants to break through the shadow and see it become lots of suns. The wall could represent a barrier put up by others—Hughes was African American, and he was **discriminated** against by white people.

There is a strong contrast between the dark shadows cast by the wall and the sunlight released at the end of the poem. Darkness suggests misery—the narrator's despondency and loss of hope. The use of exclamation marks when the speaker realizes the possibility of finding the light again powerfully expresses his frustration and desperation:

My hands!
My dark hands!
Break through the wall!
Find my dream!

A Poem for Every Dreamer

We don't know the precise nature of Hughes's dream, or the obstacle in it. This allows the poem to represent everyone with dreams who faces difficulties, gives up for a while, but then decides to keep on trying to overcome them. The poem could inspire readers to keep on battling no matter what obstacles they face, or how discouraged they have become.

LANGSTON HUGHES

1902–1967

Born: Joplin, Missouri, USA

Shortly after graduating from high school, Hughes achieved one of his dreams: having a poem published. He went on to become an increasingly successful writer. Initially, he was part of the Harlem Renaissance. This was a cultural movement of the 1920s and 1930s in which African American writers, musicians, artists, and other creative people tried to redefine what being black meant and to challenge racial stereotypes created by whites.

Did you know? Hughes's first published poem, "The Negro Speaks of Rivers," is also his most famous one.

Langston Hughes was largely raised by his grandmother, and she instilled in him a strong sense of racial pride.

Think About This
How Does This Poem Compare with "Neighbours"?

When poems share a similar theme, it is interesting to compare how the poets treat the subject. Benjamin Zephaniah's poem "Neighbours" was also about racial prejudice, but the ideas expressed are different and so the poets used different techniques.

If you are asked to compare poems, you may find it helpful to note the similarities and differences in a chart like the one below.

The important thing to remember is that when you notice differences you need to go on to think about *why* each poet made that choice, and *how* the techniques each chose helped to achieve the intended purpose of the poem.

	"As I Grew Older"	"Neighbours"
Themes/ ideas	Achieving the dream of overcoming racism takes a lot of effort. As the poet grew older and faced obstacles he gave up on his dream, but this poem marks a turning point when he finds the determination to try again.	Racism can be overcome by people living side by side so that they learn what each other are really like and stop being afraid of each other.
Form	Jazz verse that echoes the music associated with black culture.	Free verses with stanzas to clearly mark each stage in the argument.
Structure	Written in chronological (time) order.	Each stanza creates a step in his argument toward the need to overcome prejudice.
Language techniques	Repetition of images of a wall, the Sun, and darkness.	Repetition of "I."

"Do not go gentle into that good night"

In this poem, Dylan Thomas uses the energy and liveliness of a form of poem called a **villanelle** to urge his aging father to not just give up and die, but to fight against his decline. The result is a powerful expression of Thomas's feelings of rage, grief, and love.

This poem should be read aloud to hear the full impact of its powerful rhythm and sounds. You can read it aloud yourself or find recordings of it on the Internet. One of the best recordings is by the famous Welsh actor Richard Burton.

THE VILLANELLE

Traditionally, a villanelle is a six-stanza song that is danced to. It has a strong pattern of rhythm and repeated lines, which creates the liveliness needed for the dance. The first five stanzas have three lines and the last stanza has four lines.

Throughout the poem, key lines are repeated in the following pattern:

Line 1 of the first stanza is repeated as line 3 of the second stanza, as line 3 of the fourth stanza, and as line 3 of the sixth stanza. Line 3 of the first stanza is repeated as line 3 of the third stanza, line 3 of the fifth stanza, and line 4 of the sixth stanza.

"Do not go gentle into that good night"

by Dylan Thomas

Do not go gentle into that good night,
Old age should burn and rave at close of day;
Rage, rage against the dying of the light.

Though wise men at their end know dark is right,
Because their words had forked no lightning they
Do not go gentle into that good night.

Good men, the last wave by, crying how bright
Their frail deeds might have danced in a green bay,
Rage, rage against the dying of the light.

Wild men who caught and sang the sun in flight,
And learn, too late, they grieved it on its way,
Do not go gentle into that good night.

Grave men, near death, who see with blinding sight
Blind eyes could blaze like meteors and be gay,
Rage, rage against the dying of the light.

And you, my father, there on the sad height,
Curse, bless, me now with your fierce tears, I pray.
Do not go gentle into that good night.
Rage, rage against the dying of the light.

WORDS YOU MAY NOT KNOW

deeds: These are actions that are performed
consciously or intentionally.
gay: At the time the poem was written,
the word only meant cheerful.

Sounds Great…But What Does It Mean?

Begin to study the poem by noting down everything that you can understand. For example:

- The speaker is talking to someone.
- The speaker doesn't want that person to "go gentle."
- The speaker believes that old people should rage at something.

Knowing some biographical details will help you understand the poem further. Dylan Thomas wrote this poem when his elderly father was going blind and dying. Knowing this helps make sense of the three phrases "good night," "close of day," and "dying of the light"—they are all **euphemisms** for dying. They are especially relevant because they include the idea of the approaching darkness that would result from the blindness Thomas's father faced.

The main idea Thomas is expressing is the belief that his father should not just accept blindness and death but fight against it, living his last years with passion.

BUILDING THE ARGUMENT

Thomas builds this argument across the six stanzas of the poem. In each of the first five, he argues how different types of people face death. In stanza 1 it is those in "Old age"; in stanza 2 it is "wise men"; in stanza 3 "Good men"; in stanza 4 "Wild men"; and in stanza 5 "Grave men."

Alternately, these men "Rage, rage against the dying of the light" or they "Do not go gentle into that good night." In the last stanza, Thomas pleads and prays that his own father will do the same.

Now that you have gained a broad understanding of what the poem is about, you can look at each stanza more closely. Remember, all the details the poet has included will have been chosen to help express the main idea more effectively.

DYLAN THOMAS

1914–1953

Born: Swansea, Wales, UK

Dylan Thomas's first poems were published when he was 19 years old. They were an instant success because his use of **rhetoric**, imagery, and wordplay dazzled readers and critics. During his short lifetime, Thomas was a prolific writer—not just of poetry, but short stories, a play, and a film script, too. He also toured widely, giving lectures and readings. Sadly, he was also an alcoholic and he died at the age of only 39.

Did you know? Dylan Thomas had a famously troubled marriage to his wife, Caitlin Mcnamara. According to Thomas, he proposed to her the night they met!

Dylan Thomas grew up in South Wales, learning Shakespeare and poetry by heart from his beloved father.

Strong Emotions

One reason this poem is popular is because many people share the experience of seeing a beloved parent die. Readers identify with the strength of Thomas's feelings and the desperation with which he pleads with his father not to give in to death. But how does the poet make the reader feel his emotions? Which words in the first stanza do you think best express the strength of Thomas's feelings? How about "burn," "rave," and "rage"? For each of the words you choose, note down what they suggest to you.

Did you notice that these words have similar associations? This allows the ideas they carry—of anger, blazing fire, and energy—to build up and become stronger with each line. The repetition of whole lines, evocative words, and images works in the same way. The emotion they suggest builds in intensity until it reaches its climax in the final stanza.

THE POWER OF SOUNDS

Dylan Thomas used rhythm, rhyming words, and repetition. He also made extensive use of two other techniques, called alliteration and **assonance**.

Alliteration is the use of words beginning with the same sound in each stanza—for instance, "go" and "good," "though" and "their," "deeds" and "danced." Assonance is the use of words with similar vowel sounds, such as "age," "rave," "day," and "blaze."

Both techniques link words and therefore also the ideas that these words represent. The accumulation of sound strengthens the impression of how deeply Thomas grieves and how passionately he urges his father to resist death.

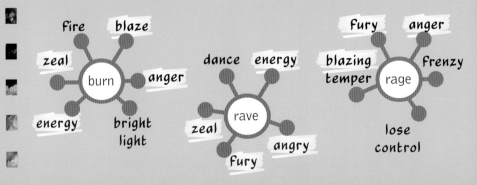

ANALYZING POETRY: POINT, EVIDENCE, EXPLAIN (P.E.E.)

Point: The poet urges his father not to give in to death.

Evidence: "Do not go gentle into that good night."

Explain: Thomas is telling his father not to become gentle and weak because then he will enter the "good night." This term might be a metaphor for death, but it could also refer to his father's oncoming blindness. Although the night is described as "good," death is still something Thomas is desperate for his father to resist—probably because he will miss him so much and cannot bear the thought of his father no longer being there.

When you are suggesting ideas that are clearly present in the text, it is fine for you to be definite about them. However, you can also be more tentative (less definite) and use words and phrases such as *possibly*, *perhaps*, *it could be*, and so on.

Image and Metaphor

In the third stanza, Thomas uses a natural image—that of waves "dancing" into a pleasantly green bay—to express how good men feel that they still have more good deeds to do. In the first line, there is a play on the word *wave* in "the last wave by" so that, in the reader's mind, waving goodbye blends with the idea that the tide is going out—another metaphor for death.

"Valentine"

On Valentine's Day, what would you hope to receive from someone who loves you? A romantic card? Chocolates? A red rose? What if that special person gave you a carefully wrapped present and inside it was...an onion?! Would you think it was a joke? What would you think they were trying to tell you with this strange present?

Before you read this poem, spend a few minutes jotting down all the similarities you can think of between being in love and an onion. Now read the poem to yourself. See whether the poet has included your ideas, and what others are present.

Ideas About Love

You will see that the version of love offered in this poem is very different from the romantic version usually celebrated on Valentine's Day. What ideas about love does the onion represent? Reread the poem and make a list before reading on.

At the beginning of the poem, we may be amused at the idea of a person being offered an onion on Valentine's Day. However, by the end of the poem, once all the comparisons are made, the reader is no longer laughing.

The love that the poet describes here seems realistic, bringing sadness as well as pleasure. Unlike the pretty flowers, cute cards, and sentimental kissograms, the love described here has an element of danger.

EXTENDED METAPHOR

When a writer uses the same object to make several comparisons about the same idea, it is called an extended metaphor. By repeatedly comparing traditional ideas of love with the onion, Carol Ann Duffy asks the reader to consider how real love is different from the romantic clichés associated with Valentine's Day.

"Valentine"
by Carol Ann Duffy

Not a red rose or a satin heart.

I give you an onion.
It is a moon wrapped in brown paper.
It promises light
like the careful undressing of love.

Here.
It will blind you with tears
like a lover.
It will make your reflection
a wobbling photo of grief.

I am trying to be truthful.

Not a cute card or a kissogram.

I give you an onion.
Its fierce kiss will stay on your lips,
possessive and faithful
as we are,
for as long as we are.

Take it.
Its platinum loops shrink to a wedding-ring,
if you like.

Lethal.
Its scent will cling to your fingers,
cling to your knife.

WORDS YOU MAY NOT KNOW

kissogram: This is a message delivered along with a kiss; it is
usually arranged as a surprise for a special occasion.

The Impact of Lines, Pauses, and Stanzas

Would Duffy's writing have the same effect on the reader if it was set out like prose? Read this version of her poem and decide for yourself:

Valentine Not a red rose or a satin heart. I give you an onion. It is a moon wrapped in brown paper. It promises light like the careful undressing of love. Here. It will blind you with tears like a lover. It will make your reflection a wobbling photo of grief. I am trying to be truthful. Not a cute card or a kissogram. I give you an onion. Its fierce kiss will stay on your lips, possessive and faithful as we are, for as long as we are. Take it. Its platinum loops shrink to a wedding-ring, if you like. Lethal. Its scent will cling to your fingers, cling to your knife.

One of the first things you might notice is that you read this prose version a lot faster. Line endings and gaps between stanzas make the reader pause.

By carefully selecting the words that are emphasized at the start and end of a line, Duffy can help readers notice her key ideas. She can also create a particular tone of voice. For example, there is something very confident in the way the writer begins mid-sentence, declaring:

Not a red rose or a satin heart.
I give you an onion

The pause between the lines makes the reader wonder for a brief moment what the poet's present will be.

The Position of "Onion"

Placing the word onion at the end of the line gives the word maximum impact. And it deserves it: an onion is not a predictable present. In fact, it sounds far worse than a red rose or satin cushion—at least they are romantic. After all that build-up, placing "onion" at the end of the line makes it like the punchline in a joke, and suggests a comic tone.

FRAGMENTS

In the poem, there are two lines made up of just one word each. These are called fragments or **minor sentences**:

> *Here*
> *Lethal*

Each of these minor sentences begins a new stanza, which makes the reader notice them more. Why does Duffy do so much to make you notice them?

The answer is that they are key words in the poem. "Here" begins the discovery of what real love is like, as the onion's layers are removed. "Lethal" is shocking and threatening. Love is not supposed to be deadly, but the final stanza suggests exactly that. It is a warning. The loved one has a knife and the power to cut up all that the onion represents, and so destroy the love the poet offers.

PURPOSE, AUDIENCE, CONTEXT, AND THEMES (PACT)

You need to make sure that the way you interpret a poem is sensible and that you are not going off in the wrong direction. To do this, you should think about the poem's Purpose, Audience, Context, and Themes, or **PACT**.

Purpose: The poet has an **intention**, and everything he or she includes is designed to help achieve this purpose—to make an argument, to describe an experience, to show a truth, and so on.

Audience: Poems are published in a particular time and culture that shapes the audience's beliefs and behavior. You need to find out about the original intended readers because their views may be very different from yours!

Context: This is the time, place, and culture in which the poet lived. It shapes the poet's view of life and the way in which he or she writes.

Themes: These are the key ideas that the poet wants to express. You can usually summarize the relevant themes in a sentence—for example, "Real love is far more complex than Valentine's Day images suggest."

A Victorian audience's ideas about love might be very different from what people think today.

CAROL ANN DUFFY

1955–

Born: Glasgow, Scotland

As a child, Carol Ann Duffy loved reading, and borrowed as many books as possible at a time from the library. She began writing poetry when she was 11 years old.

Carol Ann Duffy's poetry is very popular in the United Kingdom. She writes a lot about being a woman, and about love and relationships. But she also tackles disturbing subjects such as violence. Her poetry is often surprising and usually witty. Duffy says: "I like to use simple words but in a complicated way." To achieve this, she uses words that have more than one meaning, and phrases that are meant to remind the reader of other texts.

Did you know? Duffy is the first woman Poet Laureate in the United Kingdom. This is a traditional honorary position that is held by one celebrated British poet at a time. Past Poet Laureates include William Wordsworth and Ted Hughes.

"Sonnet 116"

This **sonnet** by William Shakespeare was written more than 400 years ago, but don't let that put you off! Shakespeare's ideas about true love are as relevant today as Duffy's views in "Valentine." Read through the poem a few times and look at the box below to find the meaning of any unfamiliar words. Use the reading and analyzing techniques that have been discussed in this book to make sense of the poem as best you can.

The key to understanding the poem is in the first few lines:

> *Let me not to the marriage of true minds*
> *Admit impediments.*

Shakespeare says he will not admit that any obstacles can come between people who are of one mind and want to be united. First he explains that this is because of what true love is *not* like. True love does not alter, even if the other person or circumstances change. It does not allow itself to be destroyed.

Instead, true love is so reliable that it can be compared to a landmark (line 5) or a star (line 7) that sailors relied on to navigate their course. True love is not made a fool of by time because it cannot be stopped by the loved one aging or dying (lines 9–11). It will last until the end of time. Shakespeare finishes by staking his reputation on what he believes. If what he says is wrong (an error) and he can be proved to be wrong, then he is not a writer nor has any man truly loved.

WORDS YOU MAY NOT KNOW

impediments: These are obstacles that can get in the way.
remover: A person who removes something is a remover.
ever-fixed mark: This is a permanent landmark that you can rely on to figure out your route.
tempests: These are violent, windy storms.
star: In the past, sailors relied on the position of the North Star to figure out their route across the ocean
bark: This is a type of ship.
fool: A professional entertainer in a medieval court was called a fool.
edge of doom: This is another way to describe the end of the world.
writ: This is an old-fashioned way of saying wrote.

"Sonnet 116"

by William Shakespeare

Let me not to the marriage of true minds
Admit impediments. Love is not love
Which alters when it alteration finds,
Or bends with the remover to remove.
O no! it is an ever-fixed mark,
That looks on tempests and is never shaken;
It is the star to every wandering bark,
Whose worth's unknown, although his height be taken.
Love's not Time's fool, though rosy lips and cheeks
Within his bending sickle's compass come;
Love alters not with his brief hours and weeks,
But bears it out even to the edge of doom.
If this be error and upon me prov'd,
I never writ, nor no man ever lov'd.

Wordplay

The first four lines of this poem are tricky to read because words and parts of words are repeated—for example:

Love is not love

How can love not be love? When part of a poem is hard to understand, go back to the sentence before it and see how it follows on. In the first sentence, what Shakespeare values is the love between "true minds"—people who are of one mind, and faithful to each other. This helps us understand the next sentence—love is not this kind of true love if it:

alters when it alteration finds,
Or bends with the remover to remove.

The words "alters" and "alteration" come from the same root word: alter (meaning to change). So true love does not change even if it finds things have altered.

Similarly "remover" and "remove" share the same root, but they also have more than one meaning: A "remover" is a person who takes something away (removes it) or who leaves (removes themselves). Shakespeare is saying that true love does not cooperate in bringing about its own destruction.

This house belonged to Shakespeare's mother.

WILLIAM SHAKESPEARE

1564–1616

Born: Stratford-upon-Avon, England

There are 154 known sonnets by Shakespeare. They were first published together in 1609. It is generally believed that in addition to his poetry, Shakespeare wrote 37 plays, all between 1590 and 1613.

William Shakespeare's father was a glove maker and wool merchant, and his mother was the daughter of a wealthy landowner. Shakespeare married Anne Hathaway, the daughter of a farmer, in 1585. They had three children within a few years.

By 1592, Shakespeare had left his family behind and moved to London. He had a patron (someone who financed his work), the Earl of Southampton, and Shakespeare dedicated his first published poems to him. He also became both an actor and playwright in the Lord Chamberlain's Company.

In the 1590s, during Queen Elizabeth I's reign, Shakespeare mostly wrote comedies and history plays—such as *A Midsummer Night's Dream*, *Much Ado About Nothing*, and *Richard III*. When James I became king in 1603, the acting company was renamed the King's Men. By then, Shakespeare was writing tragedies such as *Hamlet*, *Othello*, *King Lear*, and *Macbeth*. He moved back to Stratford-upon-Avon five years before his death in 1616.

Context: Making Sense of Shakespeare's Imagery

Poets draw on the world they know to create images that their readers will understand. For you to understand Shakespeare's images in the way his audience did, you need to know what Elizabethans believed.

Stars: In Shakespeare's time, sailing ships were exploring the world and bringing precious cargo from faraway places. Great skill was needed to follow a route across the ocean to a destination. Sailors relied on "ever-fixed marks" such as the position of churches on a coastline, and the position of the Sun and stars, to help them navigate.

The fool: A fool was another name for a jester. A jester's job was to amuse the monarch. Jesters wore brightly colored costumes that often included a three-pointed cloth hat with a jingle bell on each point. They held a mock scepter (rod carried by a king or queen) called a bauble.

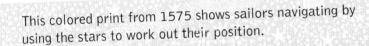

This colored print from 1575 shows sailors navigating by using the stars to work out their position.

Time: Time is described as a person carrying a sickle (a blade used to harvest crops) like the Elizabethan idea of the Grim Reaper, who represented death.

Doom: The Elizabethans were Christians. They believed that on Doomsday the world would end and God would judge everyone, sending them either to heaven or hell. Another name for this event is the Last Judgment.

The Sonnet

Shakespeare is using a traditional form of poetry called a sonnet. The sonnet has a long history of being written by a man who is expressing his love for a woman and hopes she will return his affections. The sonnet form first became popular in Italy during the Renaissance, when the poet Petrarch produced a sequence of them. They addressed an idealized woman called Laura. During Shakespeare's lifetime, poets often used the sonnet form when writing about love and romance.

In "Sonnet 116," Shakespeare adapted the Petrarchan form to suit his purposes better. He broke the 14 lines into four parts to build his argument:

Quartet 1: There should be no obstacles to true love.
Quartet 2: True love does not change.
Quartet 3: True love cannot be destroyed.
Couplet 4: If I am wrong, then I am not a writer and true love does not exist.

The division into **quartets** and **couplets** is reinforced through the rhyme scheme. Each quartet is ABAB, which means that lines 1 and 3 rhyme and lines 2 and 4 have a different rhyme. The final couplet is CC—the two lines rhyme together.

VARYING THE SONNET FORM

Shakespeare did not always write his sonnets in exactly the same way. In some of them, quartet 1 and 2 address the same question, which quartet 3 and the couplet then answer. Whatever changes Shakespeare made to the sonnet form, he always ensured that it suited the ideas he was expressing and helped him achieve his purpose.

What Have We Learned?

At the beginning of this book, you set out to explore poems written about emotions, and to learn how to read and interpret poetry. You have read a wide variety of poems by writers living in different periods, cultures, and circumstances. You have also studied a wide range of forms.

All the poets featured in this book express strong emotions in their poems—sometimes about similar themes and ideas. However, even when they write about the same issue, poets may reach different conclusions. As the poets in this book all live in different places and times, they also reflect different experiences of life. In addition, we have seen how poets choose different forms and techniques to express their ideas.

Themes

Listed below and opposite are the principle themes explored in the poems included in this book. Some of the poems focus on multiple, overlapping themes.

RACISM

In "nikki-rosa," "Neighbours," and "As I Grew Older," all three poets express anger at racism and a desire to see things change. They live on two continents and write at different times during the 20th century, yet they share the frustration of being misunderstood because of racial stereotyping by white people. Zephaniah and Giovanni's solutions are similar: the white person needs to recognize that they do not understand black people and learn to dismantle their prejudiced ideas. In contrast, Langston Hughes's solution is that he, the African American man, must never lose his dream and must fight on to overcome the obstacles he faces.

EMOTIONS AROUND GRIEVING

The emotions of sadness and anger in times of loss and grief are explored by Langston Hughes, Dylan Thomas, and Sophie Hannah. However, in each case the focus of grief is very different: a dream, a parent, and a lover, respectively. However, all of the poems express the desire to regain what is lost—and the desperate nature of the struggle to do so.

ROMANTIC LOVE

The nature of romantic love is reflected upon by Gary Soto, Sophie Hannah, and Carol Ann Duffy. However, each poem describes a different stage in the relationship: the first date in "Oranges," the deepening relationship in "Valentine," and the aftermath of a failed relationship in "Don't Say I Said." Only Gary Soto represents love as all happiness, able to overcome any difficulty—his persona is a young teenager, and perhaps this is significant. The two adult women writers express the inevitable pain and difficulty in relationships, when lovers encounter obstacles and perhaps ultimately break up.

TRUE LOVE

Ideas about what true love is, and what it is not, are discussed by Carol Ann Duffy and Shakespeare. Shakespeare argues idealistically that the union of two people in love will encounter no obstacles because true love does not change and cannot be destroyed. If this is not correct, then true love does not exist at all. In contrast, Duffy is not idealistic. She rejects the sentimental romanticism of Valentine's Day, reflecting that inevitably real love causes both pleasure and sadness.

Write Your Own Poem About Emotions

Most of the poets whose work you have read began writing when they were children. Their first efforts were almost certainly nowhere near as good as the ones in this book, but nonetheless they kept on writing poem after poem, and over time they improved.

You may have been asked to write poems in school, or you may have written some for pleasure. If you were not happy with the result, don't let that put you off from trying again. By now you know there is a lot more to writing a poem than finding words that rhyme and counting the number of syllables you put in each line. If your poem is going to be effective, then everything you include has to be there for a reason. So be prepared to spend a lot of time and energy on your poem until it is the best it can be.

Writing poetry is a bit like learning to draw or play a musical instrument. Lots of practice—and conscious effort to learn the skills— is needed if you are going to succeed. Along the way you will produce some poems you like, and some you throw in the trash. But that's fine! The only bad poem is one you don't learn from.

If all that sounds too much like hard work, try it and see how it goes. Writing poetry can be a lot of fun and very satisfying. Read the advice on the following pages and surprise yourself with what you can achieve.

Getting Started

The suggestions that follow will help you write a poem that expresses your feelings, like the ones you have read in this book. However, the advice will also help you if you want to write any other type of poem.

Tip 1. Write What You Know

All the poets in this book followed the golden rule of writing: write about what you know. They drew on personal experience so that their poetry would be genuine and truthful. You should do the same.

Try It for Yourself

Choose an emotion you have experienced strongly and want to write about. Relive it as vividly as you can, recalling its effect on every part of you. The questions below may help you to remember important details you could use in your poem:

- What set off the feeling?
- What did you experience first? How did you change?
- What did you notice while the emotion was strong?
- What happened to your body while you felt it?
- What were you like afterward?

Tip 2. Show, Don't Tell

Emotions are hard to describe because you cannot look at or touch them, unlike a cat or a tree. Instead, poets show the emotion by describing its effect on someone as they experience it—for instance, the boy in "Oranges."

Try It for Yourself

Make a rule for yourself: you can't name the emotion you are writing about. Instead you have to show its effect on several of your different senses (sight, hearing, touch, smell, taste). Start by writing two or three lines that describe your experience of the emotion—for example:

Hugging the silky cushion that does not
purr
I hear the unnecessary rattle of the cat flap door

Tip 3. Make Comparisons

Most poets use comparisons to express different aspects of emotions. For instance, when Shakespeare wanted to express the idea that true love can be relied on, he compared it to the way sailors relied on fixed landmarks and stars to navigate their ships. Langston Hughes expressed his desire to achieve his dream as smashing through a wall that blocked out the sunlight.

Try It for Yourself

Pick an emotion and then describe three objects it could be compared to, using vivid adjectives to help you. For example:

Boredom
Is a droning television
Alphabetically ordered socks
A choking gray tie

Tip 4. Don't Just State the Obvious

Everyone knows sadness makes you cry and happy people smile. The poets in this book left out these obvious expressions of emotions. Instead, they used familiar objects in an unexpected way to represent their emotions. Dylan Thomas grieves but never sheds a tear—instead, he uses the sea and stars to express his desperation. Carol Ann Duffy's onion communicates powerfully what she wants to express about real love.

Try It for Yourself

Choose an everyday object that can express two or three aspects of an emotion you want to write about. To get started, try completing this sentence several times:

[The emotion] is like [the object] because...

For example:

Fear is like a dark forest because it is lonely, unfamiliar, and overwhelming, and you feel lost inside it.

Tip 5. Create a Persona or Voice

Even when the poets in this book wrote using "I," you could not assume they were writing as themselves. Creating a persona frees a writer to go beyond what really happened and to create a poem that may tell more "truth" about the emotion. For instance, the conversation in "Don't Say I Said" is so exaggerated that it is amusing, but it also expresses the desperation that rejected people can feel.

Try It for Yourself

Could your emotion be more powerfully expressed if you changed your identity or situation? For example, would the loss of a pet cause more grief if you were an only child who had just moved to a new town where you hadn't yet made friends?

Tip 6. Writing for Readers

If you want your poem to be read by other people, then you should spend some time and effort crafting it.

Like the poems in this book, your title and first sentence should reveal your key idea and theme, so that your reader understands what you want to express. This will allow them to correctly interpret any images you use later in the poem.

Try It for Yourself

Make sure that every word, image, technique, and sentence in your poem definitely helps you express your theme and achieve your purpose. Cut out anything that does not. Keep thinking and searching for words and ideas until you are happy that every choice is the best you can use.

TOP WRITING TIPS

- To choose the best words, you may want to use a thesaurus and rhyming dictionary (you can find these on the Internet or in a library).
- Try changing around the word order in your sentences to make sure your sentence or line ends with the word you want to emphasize most.

Tip 7. Create Patterns that Help You Express Your Ideas

The poets in this book often create patterns to emphasize their points. These patterns can include:

- repeating words or sentence structures
- creating images that show the same subject
- repeating sounds at the beginning, middle, or end of words
- using only informal or formal language, or deliberately changing the style of language for effect.

Try It for Yourself

Are there any places in your poem where creating a pattern would help you express your ideas more effectively? If there are, then make those changes!

Tip 8. Always Proofread Your Poem

When you cannot think of any way to further improve your poem, leave it for a while—at least a week—without looking at it again. Then, when you come back to your poem, you can try and read it with your audience's eyes and ears instead of your own.

At that time, read it aloud several times. You could even record yourself reading it so that you can check these points:

- Does it make sense?
- Is the spelling, grammar, and punctuation helping to make your meaning clear?
- Do the rhymes or rhythms that you have created sound right?
- Does everything in your poem help you achieve your purpose and express your theme(s)?
- Are there any effects that you didn't intend and need to get rid of?

Try It for Yourself

Be prepared to work on the poem some more until you are sure it is the best you can achieve. When you are satisfied with your poem, write it up neatly and store the copy somewhere safe. You should feel really proud of your achievement after working so hard!

If you are ready, show a second copy of your poem to a friend, a member of your family, or a teacher. You could even enter it in a poetry competition!

The images and patterns of your poem can be as strange and imaginative as you like—express yourself however feels right!

Bibliography

The following works provided important sources of information for this book:

Duffy, Carol Ann. *Mean Time*. London: Anvil Press Poetry, 1993.

Giovanni, Nikki. *ego-tripping and other poems for young children*. Westport, Conn.: Lawrence Hill & Co., 1993.

Hannah, Sophie. *Selected Poems*. London: Penguin, 2006.

Hughes, Langston. *Selected Poems*. London: Serpent's Tail, 1999.

Parker, Vic. *Benjamin Zephaniah: Writers Uncovered*. London: Heinemann, 2006.

Preston, John. 'Carol Ann Duffy Interview.' *The Telegraph*. London: May 11, 2010.

Soto, Gary. *New and Selected Poems*. San Francisco: Chronicle Books, 1995.

The Book of Common Prayer (1559).

Thomas, Dylan. *Selected Poems*. London: Phoenix, 2000.

Zephaniah, Benjamin. *Propa Propaganda*. Tarset, Northumberland: Bloodaxe Books, 1996.

Glossary

alliteration repetition of the same sounds at the beginning of words within a sentence, phrase, or line of poetry

ambiguous seeming to have more than one possible meaning or interpretation

assonance effect created when words have similar vowel sounds e.g., age, rave, day; blaze, gay, rage

autobiographical related to the writer's own life

context setting or surrounding conditions that give meaning to the text

couplet two lines of verse, which usually rhyme

discriminate to treat someone unfairly because he or she is of a particular race, sexuality, nationality, religion, and so on

dyslexia learning disorder that makes it difficult to read words

euphemism mild or indirect word or phrase substituted for another that may be too blunt, harsh, or offensive

free verse form of poetry that does not have distinct patterns, and is written in the style of natural speech

imagery pictures created in your mind as you are reading

intention purpose or reason for writing

jazz poetry poetry that uses the patterns and rhythms of jazz music

metaphor literary device that draws a comparison between two seemingly unrelated things

minor sentence one-word sentence, also sometimes referred to as a fragment

monologue piece of writing or performance in which only one person or character speaks

onomatopoeia when the sound of a word echoes its meaning e.g., rustle, buzz

persona role or character created within a poem or other piece of writing

prejudiced holding views about something or someone before knowing the facts

quartet four lines of verse

repetition repeated words, phrases, or structure used to emphasize an idea

rhetoric effective or persuasive writing and speaking

rhyme words that end with the same sound, e.g., log, dog, hog

rhythm pattern of syllable stresses in a line or section of a poem

simile image in which a comparison is made using the words "as" or "like"

sonnet poem of 14 lines, usually written in iambic pentameter, with a strict rhyme pattern that divides the poem into a group of either eight lines or six lines, or three quartets and a couplet; its traditional subject is love

stanza group of related lines in a poem that may have a particular pattern

stereotype to view a group or an issue in a fixed and oversimplified way

symbol object representing something else, such as an idea, emotion, or relationship

theme subject, idea, or thought that is explored or expressed in a poem

viewpoint perspective from which a story or idea is expressed

villanelle lively dance song that follows a strict pattern of rhythm and repeated lines

Find Out More

Hopefully, reading this book is only the beginning of your interest in exploring poetry. Here are some useful resources to help you find out more.

The Poets in This Book

Gary Soto
www.garysoto.com
This is Gary Soto's official website. It tells you about the author, his career, and his books. Gary Soto encourages his readers to write to him, so there is even a contact address you can use.

Sophie Hannah
literature.britishcouncil.org/sophie-hannah
This site gives some biographical information about Sophie Hannah and discusses the poem "Don't Say I Said" in some detail.

Nikki Giovanni
www.nikki-giovanni.com
This is Nikki Giovanni's official website. It tells you about her biography, her career, her books, and the numerous awards she has won.

Benjamin Zephaniah
www.benjaminzephaniah.com
This is Benjamin Zephaniah's official website. It tells you about his life, career, books, records, performances, and politics. You can listen to him sing, and read some of his poems. He has strong political and social views (for example, he is a passionate vegetarian).

Langston Hughes
www.biography.com/people/langston-hughes-9346313
This site tells you about Langston Hughes's life and work. There is also a video you can watch about him.

Dylan Thomas
www.dylanthomas.com
This is the official website of the Dylan Thomas Centre in Wales, and it has details about his life and works.

Carol Ann Duffy
www.bbc.co.uk/schools/gcsebitesize/english_literature/poetduffy
This site helps students revise the context, language, and ideas of Carol Ann Duffy poems. It includes videos as well as web pages.

William Shakespeare
www.shakespeares-sonnets.com
This site collects all of Shakespeare's sonnets together and gives line-by-line notes and analysis.

Books

Elizabeth, Mary. *Painless Poetry*. Hauppauge, N.Y.: Barron's Educational
    Services, Inc., 2011.
This book is a good introduction to reading, analyzing, and writing poetry. It will help you overcome your fear of poetry through fun activities, brain teasers, and tips for making poetry fun.

Janeczko, Paul. *Seeing the Blue Between: Advice and Inspiration for Young Poets*.
    Somerville, Mass.: Candlewick, 2006.
Read a wealth of advice to young writers from 32 experienced poets. It contains letters and poems from these best-loved poets from around the world.

Kennedy, Caroline (selected by). *Poems to Learn by Heart*. New York: Disney
    Press, 2013.
This collection of more than a hundred poems explores deep emotions as well as ordinary experiences.

Navasky, Bruno (selected by). *Poem in Your Pocket for Young Poets*. New York:
    Amulet Books, 2011.
The poems in the book are on pages that can be neatly torn out, so you can carry around your favorite poems in your pocket and share them with family and friends.

Other Websites

www.loc.gov/poetry
The Poetry and Literature section of the Library of Congress provides numerous resources for researching poetry and discovering information about new poems and poets. The website includes webcasts and podcasts that showcase new work by contemporary poets.

www.poetryarchive.org/poetryarchive/home.do
The Poetry Archive is continually building a huge online library of poetry selected by a panel of writers and critics. Poems can be searched by poet name, title, theme, and form.

www.poetryfoundation.org
The Poetry Foundation is dedicated to stimulating interest in poetry and keeping it alive in modern culture. The site contains extensive biographies of important poets, along with examples of their work.

www.poetryoutloud.org
Poetry Out Loud is a recitation competition funded by the Poetry Foundation and the National Endowment for the Arts. The purpose of the competition is to promote the art of memorizing and reciting poetry. The website contains a large archive of selected poetry that can be searched by title or poet.

Acknowledgments
We would like to thank the following for permission to reproduce photographs: Corbis: pp. 5 (Roy McMahon), 51 (Per Winbladh); Dreamstime: pp. 32–33 (Subbotina); Getty Images: pp. 5 (AFP), 9 (Charles Hewitt), 30, 43; Shutterstock: cover (iravgustin), pp. 1 (Masson), 3 (Aaron Amat), 12 (Cardens Design), 15 (Jason Stitt), 17 (wavebreakmedia), 22–23 (Bikeworldtravel), 25 (urosr), 26 (Vladitto), 27 (advent), 28 (Igor Zh.), 30–31 (irin-k), 34–35 (isubov), 36–37 (Alan Bryant), 39 (clearimages), 41 (Subbotina Anna), 45 (Tamas Panczel – Eross), 46–47 (Andrew Roland), 51 (karelnoppe), 52 (Tadas Naujokaitis78), 53 (Africa Studio), 54–55 (R.Filip), 57 (Hannah Eckman); Superstock: pp. 10 (Glow Images), 25 (Corbis), 35 (Album/Album); Topfoto: pp. 42 (Fine Art Images/Heritage-Images), 48 (The Granger Collection); Wikimedia: pp. 20 (Brett Weinstein), 24(David Morris), 47.

Index